SPOUSE SURVIVAL

THE "HOW TO" HANDBOOK

by: Ray H. Weinrub, C.L.U.

WHAT TO DO BEFORE OR AFTER A DEATH OCCURS

PERSONAL AND FINANCIAL ORGANIZATION

THE EXTENSIVE HANDBOOK COVERING FUNERAL ARRANGEMENTS, CONTACTS TO BE MADE, AND HOW TO GET ORGANIZED. IT CONTAINS CLEAR, SIMPLE AND CONCISE INFORMATION ON INSURANCE, INVESTMENTS, TAXES, PROBATE, CASH FLOW, WILLS, TRUSTS, MEDICARE AND SOCIAL SECURITY. YOU FILL IN THE MANY FORMS WITH PERSONAL AND FINANCIAL DATA AND ADD THE LOCATION OF EACH ITEM LISTED. THERE ARE ADDITIONAL BLANK PAGES FOR YOU TO MAKE NOTES, CHANGES AND UPDATES AS NEEDED.

ACKNOWLEDGEMENTS:

Guy Wong, CPA

Morgan Johnson, Attorney

I would like to thank the following people without whose help this handbook would not have been possible.

Harriette Abels

Marlene Chernev

Mel Chernev

Harriette Schwartz

PUBLISHED BY:

RAY H. WEINRUB

P.O. BOX 254480-118

SACRAMENTO, CA. 95825

ISBN: #0-9626726-0-2

LIBRARY OF CONGRESS

CATALOG CARD NO.: 90-090151

FIRST PRINTING JUNE 1990

COVER: DESIGNED BY TERRY PETERS/NEOGRAPHIC — LAFAYETTE, CA

PRINTED IN THE UNITED STATES OF AMERICA

GOD ASKS NO MAN WHETHER HE WILL ACCEPT LIFE. THAT IS NOT THE CHOICE! YOU MUST TAKE IT.

THE ONLY CHOICE IS HOW.

Henry Ward Beecher

SPOUSE SURVIVAL HANDBOOK

TABLE OF CONTENTS

**WHEN DEATH OCCURS,
IMMEDIATE ACTION IS NEEDED.**

GETTING ORGANIZED BEFORE DEATH OCCURS, OR STARTING A NEW LIFE AFTER DEATH OCCURS.

PLANNING FOR THE FUTURE

FOREWORD

I have been in the Life Insurance business for 35 years helping people in the areas of estate and financial planning. I have come to realize that most people desperately need help when the death of a spouse takes place. After dealing with dozens of death claims and watching the surviving spouse go through the emotional upset of death, it is easy to see that chaos sets in quickly. A portion of this emotional upset occurs because the surviving spouse does not know where to begin. The survivor has to face taxes, mortgages, bills to pay, investments to manage and other urgent decisions. Nothing is ever completely organized. He or she may not be familiar with income sources, bank accounts or where important documents are located. The survivor may not even be familiar with income taxes, what information is needed to fill out forms, or when they have to be filed.

Why does this happen? The problem is that most people avoid discussing death. One spouse does not take the time to talk to the other spouse about such matters or what has to be done when he or she dies. Some may feel that the whole estate situation is too complicated to explain to their spouse.

THAT IS WHY THIS HANDBOOK WAS CREATED.

INTRODUCTION

WHY <u>YOU</u> NEED THIS HANDBOOK

Many people have tax advisors who keep their records on computers. <u>THIS HANDBOOK IS STILL NEEDED</u> in order to list the location of the many items which will be thoroughly discussed later in this book. Everyone should be aware of his or her combined assets and liabilities, and know what may happen when the death of a spouse takes place. The emotional upset escalates and life becomes more complicated if the surviving spouse <u>DOES NOT KNOW.</u>

Researching the libraries and book stores seems to establish that no one has published a guide that organizes ones' life, listing specific items and their location, and making this information available in a clear, concise, easy-to-use small handbook like this one. In a majority of marriages, one spouse does not know where records are located, and he or she would be at a loss when a death occurs.

This handbook, **SPOUSE SURVIVAL,** shows you how to become organized and how to avoid much of the trauma that will surely take place. There are specific ways to become organized so that, in the future, a great burden will be lifted from your shoulders. If your spouse has already passed away or you are divorced, this handbook will save <u>your</u> survivors time and worry.

A majority of people who take this handbook home will say that it is exactly what they need, talk about filling in the blanks,<u> but will do nothing.</u> **Don't <u>you</u> wait until it is too late! Fill out the information in this handbook NOW! It will help you put everything in order. It will not be easy, but it could save you and your**

heirs thousands of dollars. It will definitely save many hours of emotional upset.

One of the most difficult subjects to discuss is death. However, it is easier to talk about it now than to wait until you feel that you cannot talk about it at all. Now is the time to find and learn the locations of papers, prepare for future expenses, estimate the amount of monthly cash flow needed and where it will come from. There will be changes in the future; being prepared will take some of the stress out of each day. There will be many terms that you will learn to understand such as investments, limited partnerships, common and preferred stocks, K1's and 1099's. There are many types of bonds and several retirement plans such as 401K's, profit sharing, defined benefit and money purchase plans. From assets to mortgages to medicare to wills, the glossary in the appendix has a list of items that you should review so that you have a better understanding of these terms and how they apply to you.

There may be bills that are due immediately. Often, after a death, there will be bills that are unknown to you that arrive months in the future. DO NOT pay any bill unless you are sure it is due. If you are unfamiliar with the bill, call the source and request copies, clarification and possible signature verification. If you are unfamiliar with the use of a <u>check book,</u> go to your bank and have them show you how to keep check records and deposits. Learn about endorsements and other banking services including interest-bearing accounts. Your banker will be happy to explain it all to you.

Men and women need to be informed even when one or both are working. Both need to know **everything.**

Be prepared! Organize yourself with this handbook. It lists all the necessary information, location of items and papers and actions that should be taken **NOW.**

If there has been a recent death, you can fill out information in this handbook to help get things organized. Once this handbook with its attached notes and information has been filled out, put it in a safe place. Do not use a safe deposit box unless you check with the institution to be sure that the box will not be sealed upon a death. Notify a close family member or heir that this handbook exists and where it is located. You should also give this information to one or more members of your financial help team. Make a memo to yourself to review and update changes that take place in the future. This handbook will help married couples, widows, widowers, divorcees or other single people.

Age makes no difference; the older you are, the more your heirs need to know, especially when a death occurs. By filling out this handbook, you do not have to inform your children or heirs what your assets consist of while you are alive. Tell them the location of this handbook so they can easily assemble the assets and liabilities of the estate eliminating the confusion which would occur if it did not exist. This can save many hundreds of dollars in attorney and tax advisor fees.

Get a pencil out now so you can start to fill in the indicated areas as you come to them. Many of the left pages of this handbook are blank so you can easily make notes, comments, updates and changes.

WHEN DEATH OCCURS, IMMEDIATE ACTION IS NEEDED.

CHAPTER I   FIRST PRIORITIES

A. Funeral Home

If no prior arrangements have been made, call the funeral home or have a close relative or friend do it for you. Arrange for the funeral service and provide the funeral director with the information needed for the obituary notice to be placed in the newspaper. Be sure to specify where memorial donations should be sent.

B. Notifying Friends and Relatives

Notify relatives, friends and business associates. If you can, ask them to make calls to others for you. If there are small children, special arrangements for their care should be made as soon as possible.

C. Meeting with Clergy

Talk to the funeral director and clergy to discuss the type of service desired. Pick out the casket, arrange for flowers and obtain at least a dozen certified copies of the death certificate.

This is an emotional time; allow people to help you. The funeral director can provide you with information regarding the goods and services needed and their costs.

D. Safe Deposit Box

If you have a safe deposit box, remove the Will so you have it available when you see your attorney. There may be other items you wish to remove at the same time. Many bank rules now state that anyone named on the box has free access even if others named on the box are deceased. Check with your bank to be sure the box is not sealed when a death occurs.

E. Professional Help Team Listed

Contact the people on your Professional Help Team as listed in Chapter III. Sample letters are located in Chapter IV, so you can notify insurance companies, Social Security Administration and others.

F. Pall Bearers Listed

You now have to decide whom you wish to serve as pall bearers. If death has not taken place see Chapter XIV (page 87).

1. _____

2. _____

3. _____

4. _____

5. _____

6. _____

CHAPTER II   CONTACTS TO BE MADE

A. Military Organization

If either you or your spouse is now or were ever in the military, your funeral director has Veterans Administration forms and can help you prepare them. You should contact the Veterans Administration if the deceased was retired military, active military or a veteran. For life insurance have a policy number available. If there are children between the ages of 18 and 25, there may be benefits under the War Orphans and Widows Assistance Act. If possible, be sure you have the branch of service, serial number and discharge papers of the deceased.

B. Fraternal, Service Clubs

If either spouse belongs to a fraternal organization or service club (Shrine, Veterans, Elks, Kiwanis or Rotary) you should check now on any possible benefits or services that might be available. Many of them help with the funeral arrangements and possibly provide pall bearers.

C. Civil Service

Check Civil Service benefits if the deceased died in service after 18 months on the job, was married 2 years and had children or was disabled. Forms may be filed at any federal agency or appropriate Civil Service Bureau. See the sample letter in Chapter IV (page 25).

D. Social Security

Call your local Social Security office. A covered worker whose surviving spouse is over age 60 is eligible for benefits. If there are minor children, there are additional benefits. If you are covered under the Social Security program, you still need to check with them on possible changes in your current benefits.

E. Life Insurance

Contact your life insurance agent or each insurance company individually. You need the policy numbers. Enter all policy information on page 47 so it is always available for quick reference.

Most companies will let you leave the death benefit proceeds on deposit earning interest until you make up your mind what you want to do. A certified copy of the death certificate is required. You **DO NOT** need nor do you have to pay an attorney or anyone else to help you receive death proceeds from life insurance. Do not forget to change the beneficiary designation on your own policies.

F. Employer

Even if self-employed, there may be company benefits available. You should also check all previous employers for possible benefits. See the designated person of the firm about life insurance benefits, disability benefits, 401K investment plans and retirement plans. Find out NOW about health and disability insurance and whether continuation or conversion is possible.

G. Social Organizations

Social organizations, unions, auto clubs and professional organizations may have some benefits. There may even be some club ownership (Country Club, Tennis Club, etc.), that can be sold or continued. Check your rights. Do not make decisions regarding sales of memberships for at least six months.

H. Older Americans Act

There is a variety of services funded by the <u>Older Americans Act</u> which are available in each community through the Area Agency On Aging. These services which are available to all older persons include information and referral on where to get help, emergency numbers for crisis, transportation, homemaking and maintenance (including laundry, shopping, errands and more), medical equipment, nutrition and meal delivery, adult day care services, counseling, support groups and even social and recreational activities. You may buy a copy of the booklet called "Where To Turn For Help For Older Persons" from the Superintendent of Documents, U.S. Government Printing Office, Washington, D.C. 20402

I. Bank and S & L Accounts
Try to locate all bank accounts. If there is a bank account and it cannot be found, some State laws say that any account that goes for 5 years with no activity will be turned over to that state. Call the IRS and see if they can help you, as all accounts with interest over $10 must be reported to the IRS by the bank.

J. Utility Services
You may want to change the name on all the utilities. You should also familiarize yourself with the location of the main home gas and water cut-off, electrical fuses or circuit breakers. Know who services your alarm system. Learn how to open the garage door if the automatic opener is not working. Find out the garbage collection day, how to contact the gardener, who handles the pest control and how often these services are performed. Find out where to have the fire extinguisher serviced.

START NOW BY FILLING IN YOUR PROFESSIONAL HELP TEAM CHART ON THE FOLLOWING PAGES.

NOTES, CHANGES AND UPDATES

CHAPTER III   PROFESSIONAL HELP TEAM

ATTORNEY

NAME_____FIRM_____

ADDRESS_____

CITY_____STATE_____ZIP_____

PHONE_____

ACCOUNTANT

NAME_____FIRM_____

ADDRESS_____

CITY_____STATE_____ZIP_____

PHONE_____

INSURANCE AGENTS (LIFE, HEALTH, GENERAL)

NAME_____FIRM_____

ADDRESS_____

CITY_____STATE_____ZIP_____

PHONE_____

NAME_____FIRM_____

ADDRESS_____

CITY_____STATE_____ZIP_____

PHONE_____

NAME_____FIRM_____

ADDRESS_____

CITY_____STATE_____ZIP_____

PHONE_____

NOTES, CHANGES AND UPDATES

PHYSICIAN OR HMO   (HUSBAND)

HMO #_____

NAME_____FIRM_____

ADDRESS_____

CITY_____STATE_____ZIP_____

PHONE_____Claim form location and

where to be sent_____

_____

PHYSICIAN OR HMO   (WIFE)

HMO #_____

NAME_____FIRM_____

ADDRESS_____

CITY_____STATE_____ZIP_____

PHONE_____Claim form location and

where to be sent_____

_____

DENTIST   (HUSBAND)

NAME_____FIRM_____

ADDRESS_____

CITY_____STATE_____ZIP_____

PHONE_____Claim form location and

where to be sent_____

_____

NOTES, CHANGES AND UPDATES

DENTIST   (WIFE)

NAME_____FIRM_____

ADDRESS_____

CITY_____STATE_____ZIP_____

PHONE_____Claim form location and

where to be sent_____

_____

FINANCIAL PLANNER

NAME_____FIRM_____

ADDRESS_____

CITY_____STATE_____ZIP_____

PHONE_____

INVESTMENT BROKER

NAME_____FIRM_____

ADDRESS_____

CITY_____STATE_____ZIP_____

PHONE_____

BANKER

NAME_____FIRM_____

ADDRESS_____

CITY_____STATE_____ZIP_____

PHONE_____

NOTES, CHANGES AND UPDATES

TRUST OFFICER

NAME_____FIRM_____

ADDRESS_____

CITY_____STATE_____ZIP_____

PHONE_____

VETERINARIAN

NAME_____FIRM_____

ADDRESS_____

CITY_____STATE_____ZIP_____

PHONE_____

NOTES, CHANGES AND UPDATES

CHAPTER IV   SAMPLE LETTERS

TO LIFE INSURANCE COMPANIES

DATE

NAME
COMPANY
ADDRESS
CITY   STATE   ZIP

REF: (INSURED NAME AND POLICY NUMBER)

TO: DEATH CLAIMS DEPARTMENT

This is to advise you that my husband (wife) passed away on (month, day, year) at (location). Cause of death was (as listed on death certificate). Please send me the correct forms for filling out claims on his (her) insurance. As beneficiary I would like all the information on every settlement option. Please search your files for any other policies the insured may have had.

Sincerely,

NAME
ADDRESS
CITY, STATE, ZIP
PHONE

TO THE SOCIAL SECURITY ADMINISTRATION

CALL FIRST AS THEY ARE VERY HELPFUL

DATE
(ADDRESS THE LOCAL OFFICE)

REF: NAME AND SOCIAL SECURITY NUMBER

To whom it may concern:

My husband (wife) died on (date), (location). As the named beneficiary I would like to schedule an appointment. Please let me know what documents you will need other than the death certificate.

Sincerely,

(YOUR NAME AND COMPLETE ADDRESS)
(ALSO YOUR SOCIAL SECURITY NUMBER)

TO CIVIL SERVICE

DATE
CIVIL SERVICE COMMISSION
1900 E ST., N.W.
WASHINGTON, D.C. 20415
(PHONE 202-632-7700)

REF: DECEASED NAME

To whom it may concern:

My husband (wife) died on (date), (location). As the named beneficiary I would like to receive the forms necessary to file a claim. Please let me know what documents will be needed in addition to the death certificate.

Sincerely,

(YOUR NAME AND COMPLETE ADDRESS)
(ALSO YOUR SOCIAL SECURITY NUMBER)

A similar letter can be composed and sent out to whomever you wish. The main thing is to give the name, number, if any, and a complete address. A phone number would be very important. Additional addresses are on the next two pages.

INTERNAL REVENUE SERVICE

If you live in:	Use this address:
Florida, Georgia, South Carolina	Atlanta, GA 39901
New Jersey, New York (New York City and counties of Nassau, and Westchester)	Holtsville, NY 00501
New York (all other counties), Connecticut, Maine, Massachusetts, New Hampshire, Rhode Island, Vermont	Andover, MA 05501
Illinois, Iowa, Minnesota, Missouri, Wisconsin	Kansas City, MO 64999
Delaware, District of Columbia, Maryland, Pennsylvania, Virginia	Philadelphia, PA 19255
Indiana, Kentucky, Michigan, Ohio, West Virginia	Cincinnati, OH 45999
Kansas, New Mexico, Oklahoma, Texas	Austin, TX 73301
Alaska, Arizona, California (counties of Alpine, Amador, Butte, Calaveras, Colusa, Contra Costa, Del Norte, El Dorado, Glenn, Humboldt, Lake, Lassen, Marin, Mendocino, Modoc, Napa, Nevada, Placer, Plumas, Sacramento, San Joaquin, Shasta, Sierra, Siskiyou, Solano, Sonoma, Sutter, Tehama, Trinity, Yolo, and Yuba), Colorado, Idaho, Montana, Nebraska Nevada, North Dakota, Oregon, South Dakota, Utah, Washington, Wyoming	Ogden, UT 84201
California (all other counties), Hawaii	Fresno, CA 93888
Alabama, Arkansas, Louisiana, Mississippi, North Carolina, Tennessee	Memphis, TN 37501
American Samoa	Philadelphia, PA 19255
Guam	Commissioner of Revenue and Taxation 855 West Marine Dr. Agana, GU 96910
Puerto Rico (or if excluding income under section 933) Virgin Islands: Nonpermanent residents	Philadelphia, PA 19255
Virgin Islands: Permanent residents	V.I. Bureau of Internal Revenue Lockhards Garden No. 1A Charlotte Amalie, St. Thomas, VI 00802
Foreign country: U.S. citizens and those filing Form 2555 or Form 4563	Philadelphia, PA 19255
All A.P.O. or F.P.O. addresses	Philadelphia, PA 19255

RAILROAD RETIREMENT
844 RUSH ST.
CHICAGO, ILLINOIS 60611

SOCIAL SECURITY MAIN OFFICE
6400 SECURITY BLVD.
BALTIMORE, MARYLAND 21335

U.S. DEPT OF HEALTH AND HUMAN SERVICES
SOCIAL SECURITY ADMINISTRATION
WESTERN PROGRAM SERVICE CENTER
P.O. BOX 2072
RICHMOND, CALIFORNIA 94802

VETERANS ADMINISTRATION
EASTERN U.S.A.
500 WISSAHICKON AVE.
PHILADELPHIA, PENNSYLVANIA 19010

VETERANS ADMINISTRATION
WESTERN U.S.A.
FORT SNELLING
ST. PAUL, MINNESOTA 55111

FRATERNAL ORGANIZATIONS SHOULD
HAVE LOCAL ADDRESSES.

GETTING ORGANIZED BEFORE DEATH OCCURS, OR STARTING A NEW LIFE AFTER DEATH OCCURS.

CHAPTER V.   HOW TO GET STARTED

WARNING! IF YOU PUT THIS HANDBOOK AND ITS INFORMATION INTO A COMPUTER, YOU SHOULD STILL MAINTAIN A CURRENT HANDBOOK! THIS WILL PROTECT YOU IN THE EVENT OF A COMPUTER ERASURE OF ALL DATA!

If both spouses are alive, sit down together and go through this handbook. In most families one spouse usually pays the bills, deposits checks and keeps track of the family budget. Some split the responsibility by one paying the house bills and the other the social and other expenses. To begin, each spouse should take the list for which he or she is responsible and fill it out. Compare the entries, fill in any blanks, use guidelines shown, and you will quickly have all the information organized and up to date.

If you are single, divorced, a widow or widower, you should still fill out the handbook to become organized. If the death of a spouse was recent, this booklet will relieve some of the pressure by showing document location and values of many estate items.

Make a list of the professionals who can be called upon when needed. Fill in the area in Chapter III with their names, addresses and phone numbers. Those who own part or all of a business need other information that should be gathered and put on a separate page. See the accountant, chief financial officer or comptroller of the business for help. Can you take over and run the business? Will it have to be sold? Become involved so you know what is going on, to enable you to make intelligent decisions. Be sure to gather all bills and list them according to whether they are due monthly, quarterly, semi-annually or annually. You will need this information for Chapter XII on cash flow expenditures.

Keep all tax related paid bills for 60 months and keep all income tax returns forever. Even though the federal statute of limitations for substantiating back-up records is three years, you should retain them for at least five years. Consult your tax advisor about your record keeping for tax purposes. See last year's income tax form, or get a copy from your accountant, to use as a guide in composing a list of all the supportive items you will need. It will help you to organize and fill in many areas of this handbook.

If you or your spouse was (or is) a pack rat, <u>NOW IS THE TIME TO THROW OUT ITEMS NOT NEEDED.</u> Keep paperwork regarding home improvement items, large purchase sales slips, etc., but you may want to throw out old bills and records that are now over 5 years old. Your record keeping starts on the next page.

START FILLING IT IN NOW!

NOTES, CHANGES AND UPDATES

CHAPTER VI   PERSONAL INFORMATION AND DOCUMENT LOCATION

THESE RECORDS UPDATED ON

(_____)

MALE NAME_____

BIRTHDATE_____

MOTHER'S MAIDEN NAME_____

SOCIAL SECURITY NO._____

DRIVER'S LICENSE NO._____

MILITARY NO._____

DISCHARGE PAPERS LOCATED_____

PASSPORT NO._____

LOCATION_____

EMPLOYER_____

FEMALE NAME_____

BIRTHDATE _____

MAIDEN NAME_____

MOTHER'S MAIDEN NAME_____

SOCIAL SECURITY NO._____

DRIVER'S LICENSE NO._____

MILITARY NO._____

DISCHARGE PAPERS LOCATED_____

PASSPORT NO._____

LOCATION_____

EMPLOYER_____

NOTES, CHANGES AND UPDATES

DATE OF MARRIAGE_____

CERTIFICATE LOCATED_____

CEMETERY NAME_____

ADDRESS_____

PLOT NO._____

RELIGIOUS AFFILIATION_____

FUNERAL DIRECTOR_____

ADDRESS_____

VEHICLE: YEAR AND MAKE_____

PINK SLIP LOCATION_____

VEHICLE: YEAR AND MAKE_____

PINK SLIP LOCATION_____

BANK_____CHECKING ACCT. NO._____

ADDRESS_____

CHECK BOOK LOCATION_____

BANK_____SAVINGS ACCT. NO._____

ADDRESS_____

PASS BOOK LOCATION_____

BANK_____CD ACCT. NO._____

ADDRESS_____

TERM_____INTEREST RATE_____

PASS BOOK LOCATION_____

SAFE DEPOSIT BOX LOCATION_____

KEYS LOCATED_____NO._____

(See "additional notes and information"

for list of box items)

NOTES, CHANGES AND UPDATES

CREDIT UNION NAME_____ACCT. NO._____

ADDRESS_____

PAPERS OR BOOK LOCATION_____

CLUB MEMBERSHIPS (Golf, Tennis, etc.)

NAME_____CARD NO._____

ADDRESS_____

NAME_____CARD NO._____

ADDRESS_____

COPYRIGHTS, PATENTS,

TRADEMARK PAPERS LOCATION_____

COIN COLLECTION LOCATION_____

APPROXIMATE VALUE_____

(Make note on opposite page as to the suggested disposition on death.)

STAMP COLLECTION LOCATED_____

APPROXIMATE VALUE_____

(Make note on opposite page as to the suggested disposition on death.)

CREDIT CARDS:_____NO._____

EMERGENCY TELEPHONE NO._____

CREDIT CARDS:_____NO._____

EMERGENCY TELEPHONE NO._____

NOTES, CHANGES AND UPDATES

CREDIT CARDS:_____NO._____
EMERGENCY TELEPHONE NO._____

CREDIT CARDS:_____NO._____
EMERGENCY TELEPHONE NO._____

CREDIT CARDS:_____NO._____
EMERGENCY TELEPHONE NO._____

DEED KIND:_____LOCATION_____
DEED KIND:_____LOCATION_____
(Make any important notes on opposite page)

DEPARTMENT STORE NAMES & CREDIT CARDS:
NAME_____CARD NO._____
NAME_____CARD NO._____
NAME_____CARD NO._____

DEFERRED COMPENSATION PLAN:_____
ORGANIZATION:_____

401K INVESTMENT PLAN_____
COMPANY CONTRIBUTION_____SELF_____

IRA ACCOUNT NO._____NAME_____
ADDRESS_____
TYPE_____ANNUAL CONTRIBUTION_____
RECORD LOCATION_____

NOTES, CHANGES AND UPDATES

KEOGH ACCT. NO._____NAME_____

ADDRESS_____

TYPE_____RECORDS LOCATION_____

_____

JOINT VENTURE AGREEMENTS_____

LOCATION_____

(Use opposite page for notes)

MORTGAGES & REAL ESTATE:_____

ADDRESS_____

DEED NAME:_____

MORTGAGE POLICY NO.:_____PREMIUM:_____

MORTGAGE POLICIES LOCATED_____

PREVIOUS HOME PAPERS LOCATED _____

_____

LEASE AGREEMENTS & LOCATION:_____

_____

_____

NOTES PAYABLE_____

TO WHOM_____

ADDRESS_____

DUE DATE_____INTEREST_____

PERIOD_____LOCATION_____

NOTES, CHANGES AND UPDATES

NOTES RECEIVABLE_____

FROM WHOM_____

ADDRESS_____

DUE DATE_____INTEREST_____

PERIOD_____LOCATION_____

OTHER PENSION AND RETIREMENT PLANS

NAME_____TYPE_____

PAPER LOCATION_____

OTHER INFORMATION:_____

SECURITIES AND INVESTMENTS:
(Make a sheet on each one)

COMPANY_____CERTIFICATE NO._____

PURCHASE DATE_____

TYPE: COMMON_____PREFERRED_____

BONDS_____

DEBENTURE_____MUTUAL FUND_____

MONEY MARKET_____MUNI. BOND_____

(Describe in greater detail on note page)

LIMITED OR OTHER PARTNERSHIPS_____

CERT. NO._____NO. SHARES_____@_____

TOTAL PRICE_____

LOCATION OF CERTIFICATE_____

BROKER_____FIRM_____

PHONE_____

(Put additional notes on opposite page)

NOTES, CHANGES AND UPDATES

PETS: TYPE_____NAME_____

VET_____SHOTS DUE_____

TYPE_____NAME_____

VET_____SHOTS DUE_____

Social security information: (list retirement, medicare, any disability information, claims pending, etc. Use opposite page or put on separate sheet and make note of information location.)

TRUSTS:

FAMILY REVOCABLE NO._____REG. DATE_____

CHILDREN'S TRUSTS:_____

LIVING TRUSTS:_____

TESTAMENTARY TRUSTS:_____

TRUST PAPERS ARE ALL LOCATED_____

CURRENT YEAR'S TAX PAPERS AND RECORDS
LOCATED_____

PREVIOUS YEAR'S RECORDS LOCATED:_____

_____

WILLS ARE LOCATED:_____

LAST UPDATE_____

ATTORNEY_____

ADDRESS_____

CODICIL ADDED_____

NOTES, CHANGES AND UPDATES

ADDITIONAL NOTES ON ITEM LOCATION

SALARY CHECK STUBS _____

COMMISSION STATEMENTS_____

OTHER INCOME STATEMENTS_____

(Make notes on opposite page of any additional items and location)

ALARM CO._____PERMIT NO._____

ADDRESS_____PHONE_____

LARGE ITEM PURCHASE: Instruction Booklet Location

1. REFRIGERATOR, STOVE, ETC._____
2. WASHER & DRYER _____
3. COMPUTERS_____
4. TV'S & VCR'S_____
5. SERVICE CONTRACTS_____
6. FURNITURE_____
7. MISC. PAID BILLS_____
8. AIR COND. & HEATING_____
9. CARPET & WALLPAPER_____
10. LANDSCAPE ITEMS_____

SAFE DEPOSIT BOX ITEMS:

BOX NO._____

_____   _____

_____   _____

_____   _____

NOTES, CHANGES AND UPDATES

CHAPTER VII   INFORMATION CHARTS

A. LIFE INSURANCE

COMPANY_____POLICY NO._____

ADDRESS_____

AGENT_____PHONE_____

TYPE _____FACE AMT._____

PREMIUM AMT._____DUE DATE_____

OWNER_____BENEFICIARY_____

LOAN_____RIDERS_____

COMPANY_____POLICY NO._____

ADDRESS_____

AGENT_____PHONE_____

TYPE_____FACE AMT._____

PREMIUM AMT._____DUE DATE_____

OWNER_____BENEFICIARY_____

LOAN_____RIDERS_____

B. ANNUITIES

COMPANY_____POLICY NO._____

ADDRESS_____

AGENT_____PHONE_____

TYPE_____ORIG. AMT._____

OWNER_____BENEFICIARY_____

INT. RATE_____HOW LONG_____

NOTES, CHANGES AND UPDATES

C. HEALTH PLAN

COMPANY_____POLICY NO._____

ADDRESS_____

AGENT_____PHONE_____

TYPE_____DEDUCTIBLE_____

PREMIUM AMT._____DUE DATE_____

COVERAGE DESCRIPTION_____

_____

COMPANY_____POLICY NO._____

ADDRESS_____

AGENT_____PHONE_____

TYPE_____DEDUCTIBLE_____

PREMIUM AMT._____DUE DATE_____

COVERAGE DESCRIPTION_____

_____

D. AUTO INSURANCE: FIRST VEHICLE

COMPANY_____POLICY NO._____

ADDRESS_____

AGENT_____PHONE_____

PREMIUM AMT._____DUE DATE_____

CAR_____DRIVER_____

PLPD*_____COLLISION DED.*_____

COMP*_____DED._____MED.*_____

T & L*_____RENTAL_____UMBRELLA_____

NOTES, CHANGES AND UPDATES

D. AUTO INSURANCE: SECOND VEHICLE

COMPANY_____POLICY NO._____

ADDRESS_____

AGENT_____PHONE_____

PREMIUM AMT._____DUE DATE_____

CAR_____DRIVER_____

PLPD*_____COLLISION DED.*_____

COMP*_____DED._____MED.*_____

T & L*_____RENTAL_____UMBRELLA_____

* PLPD = PERSONAL LIABILITY & PROPERTY DAMAGE
* DED. = DEDUCTIBLE
* COMP = COMPREHENSIVE
* MED. = MEDICAL
* T & L = TOWING AND LABOR

E. HOMEOWNER'S INSURANCE

COMPANY_____POLICY NO._____

ADDRESS_____

PREMIUM AMT.*_____DUE DATE_____

TYPE_____DEDUCTIBLE_____

PLPD*_____USE LOSS_____MED.*_____

FLOOD_____EARTHQUAKE_____WRK. COMP._____

NOTES, CHANGES AND UPDATES

PERSONAL PROPERTY SCHEDULE:

JEWELRY AMT._____CAMERA AMT._____

ART_____GUNS_____STAMPS_____

COINS_____SPORTS EQUIPMENT_____

OTHER_____

F. VACATION HOME INSURANCE

COMPANY_____POLICY NO._____

ADDRESS_____

PREMIUM AMT._____DUE DATE_____

TYPE_____DEDUCTIBLE_____

PLPD*_____USE LOSS_____MED.*_____

FLOOD_____EARTHQUAKE_____WRK. COMP.*_____

PERSONAL PROPERTY SCHEDULE:

JEWELRY AMT._____CAMERA AMT._____

ART_____GUNS_____STAMPS_____

COINS_____SPORTS EQUIPMENT_____

OTHER_____

* AMT. = AMOUNT
* MED. = MEDICAL
* PLPD = PERSONAL LIABILITY PROPERTY DAMAGE
* WRK. COMP = WORKMANS COMPREHENSIVE

NOTES, CHANGES AND UPDATES

G. COMPUTER OR OTHER INSURANCE

COMPANY_____POLICY NO._____

ADDRESS_____

ITEM COVERED_____

PREMIUM AMT._____DUE DATE_____

TYPE_____DEDUCTIBLE_____

PLPD_____USE LOSS_____MED._____

FLOOD_____EARTHQUAKE_____WRK. COMP._____

CHAPTER VIII   FIXED AND LIQUID ASSETS

<u>FIXED ASSETS</u>

The single largest item most people own is real estate. Record keeping is essential! You must have basic cost facts. If your current home is the second or third main residence that you have owned, you should have records of the previous home costs, improvements, and purchase and sales items that are listed on the escrow papers. If you do not have these facts, then you must try to reconstruct those figures **right now**. Try to find as many improvement cost items and bills as you can so that you can increase the cost basis of each home.

READ THIS PORTION CAREFULLY AND THEN CHECK WITH YOUR TAX ADVISOR TO FIND OUT WHERE YOU FIT INTO THE TAX SITUATION.

As the years pass most of us sell one home and buy another one. Some may do this several times during their lifetime. It is critical that you keep records on the purchase and sale of each home during your lifetime. You should also keep costs of improvements and sales and closing costs. This helps you increase your home cost basis for tax purposes. If you sold your first home and bought a new one for less money, there could be a taxable gain due on the difference. If you bought the new home within twenty-four months of the sale for more than the sales price of the first home, you can defer any profit from the sale of the first home to reduce the tax basis of the second (new) home. When you sell again you have a similar situation. You can again defer any tax liability if your new home costs more and the new purchase occurs within twenty-four months of the sale of the last home.

You can only defer the taxable gain if you bought and sold a home once within a twenty-four month period of the sale of the previous home. If you are over age 55 when a situation such as this takes place, and you are not buying a new home for more than your last one, you may qualify for and take advantage of the $125,000 tax exclusion. To qualify for this tax exemption, this home must have been your principal residence for a total of at least 3 years during the 5 year period ending on the date of the sale of the residence. It does not make any difference if you have a mortgage balance. Since this tax advantage can only be used once, never use only a portion of the $125,000. If you do, the remainder of the deduction is lost forever.

Here is an example.

Assume you bought your home for $60,000 and today it is worth $250,000. That is a $190,000 profit. If you can show you put in $20,000 of improvements, your profit is reduced to $170,000. By deducting the $125,000 exclusion, only $45,000 would be taxable. Married couples can only take the $125,000 exclusion once. If either spouse took the tax exclusion in a previous marriage, they **cannot** claim another exclusion with the new spouse. However, if two unmarried parties who have each already used the deduction, subsequently marry, the government cannot recapture the tax on the gain previously excluded by either one. Vacation or second homes do not enjoy any exclusions from taxable gains.

There is one more area to consider when talking about taxes on the sale of a home.

If you are a surviving spouse, you may qualify for a **stepped up cost basis** to the fair market value at the time of your spouse's death. This is possible if the property is held as community property or if you live in a community property state. Using the above example for community property, each spouse owns one half of the total current value of $250,000. Upon a death, both the deceased's share and the surviving spouse's share gets a stepped up cost basis of $125,000. Thus, if the home sells for $250,000 within the year of the death, there would be no tax liability. In this example, the $125,000 one time tax exclusion would not have to be used. If the surviving spouse decides to keep the home and sell at a later time, assuming a sales price of $375,000, then the stepped-up cost basis at time of death ($250,000) plus the $125,000 one time tax exclusion could be used and, thus, there would be <u>NO TAX.</u>

If the property is held as joint tenants, only the decedent's half gets a stepped up cost basis. Using the previous example, when the house sells for $250,000, the decedent's one half has a new cost basis of $125,000 and the survivor has a cost basis of $40,000 (one half the original cost of $60,000 plus one half of the $20,000 of improvements). The total cost basis under the joint tenancy now becomes $165,000. The survivor would have to pay tax on $85,000 or use the $125,000 one time tax exclusion. If the survivor waited and sold at $375,000, the cost basis of $165,000 plus the $125,000 one time tax exclusion comes to $290,000 and there would still be a tax on $85,000. This example shows why it is important to hold any asset that has growth potential as community property.

Caution. This entire area can be complex, so check with your tax advisor.

LIQUID ASSETS

Assessment of liquid assets is an area that takes much work and research if you haven't organized yourself before this time. This is the area where much of the daily and monthly paperwork takes place. Many documents are misplaced or lost over the years. That is why you need to fill in the personal information in this handbook **NOW!**

The next chapter will refresh your memory as to some of the additional items that come under the asset heading. It is shown as part of the net worth statement.

NOTES, CHANGES AND UPDATES

CHAPTER IX   NET WORTH

(AS OF:)

A. ASSETS   WHAT IS YOURS

RESIDENCE MARKET VALUE $_____

2ND HOME MARKET VALUE $_____

OTHER REAL ESTATE VALUE $_____

COMMERCIAL PROPERTY $_____

OFFICE EQUIPMENT $_____

BUSINESS VALUE
   (Incl. Goodwill) $_____

FURNISHINGS & APPLIANCES $_____

PERSONAL PROPERTY $_____

STAMP & COIN COLLECTIONS $_____

SOCIAL & COUNTRY CLUB
   MEMBERSHIPS $_____

AUTOMOBILES
   (Blue Book Value) $_____

LMTD. PARTNERSHIP
   INVESTMENTS $_____

JOINT VENTURES

ART ITEMS $_____

CASH ON HAND $_____

CHECKING & SAVINGS
   ACCOUNTS $_____

BANK CD'S, TREASURY BILLS $_____

NOTES, CHANGES AND UPDATES

CREDIT UNION ACCOUNT $_____

STOCK & BOND PORTFOLIO $_____

MUTUAL FUNDS $_____

IRA & KEOGH (HR10) ACCOUNT $_____

LIFE INS. & ANNUITY VALUES $_____

U.S. SAVINGS BONDS $_____

PENSION OR PROFIT SHARING
   PLANS $_____

DEFERRED COMPENSATION
   PLANS $_____

401 K INVESTMENT ACCOUNT $_____

DEFERRED COMMISSIONS $_____

NOTES DUE $_____

OTHER $_____

ESTIMATED TOTAL ALL ASSETS $_____

NOTES, CHANGES AND UPDATES

B. LIABILITIES   WHAT YOU OWE.

MORTGAGE BALANCE
   MAIN RESIDENCE $_____

SECOND HOME MORTGAGE
   BALANCE $_____

COMMERCIAL PROPERTY $_____

OTHER REAL ESTATE
   BALANCE $_____

INSURANCE POLICY LOANS $_____

NOTES OR PERSONAL LOANS $_____

BUSINESS LIABILITIES $_____

VISA, MASTER CARD,
   AMER. EXPRESS $_____

AUTO LOAN $_____

DEPARTMENT STORES $_____

TAXES OWED $_____

OTHER $_____

ESTIMATED LIABILITIES $_____

C. ESTIMATED NET WORTH

(ASSETS MINUS LIABILITIES) $_____

CHAPTER X   INCOME

Gathering income and expense items is another pains-taking task you will have to perform. This is especially true if there are a number of income sources. The next chapter lists items to remind you of areas regarding income and expenditures. It is difficult to make and keep a budget, so you will have to learn the source of your income and what the regular expenditures are. You can then prepare for emergencies, vacations, education and even savings. This is called CASH FLOW. If you have set up a Family Revocable Living Trust, (see Chapter XIII) you will relieve yourself of many hours of paperwork and frustration in transferring ownership when one spouse dies. Ownership of property, autos, investments, tax shelters and other assets may require name changes without this type of trust.

If you are not experienced in record keeping, now is the time to learn. If you are a surviving spouse who is still working, remember that records must be kept on all paycheck deductions. The company may not give you a 1099 (income statement form) for labor or commissions earned under $600. Be sure to report all income whether you receive a 1099 form or not. If you are married and filing jointly, and your modified adjusted income (income less deductions), plus all tax-exempt interest, is over $32,000 which includes one-half of your social security income, then that one-half social security income is also taxable.

If the deceased spouse had an IRA, it can be rolled over tax free to an IRA of the surviving spouse. You may be able to leave 401K dollars, annuities or other plans intact until needed.

SAVE MONEY NOW, SO YOU WILL HAVE SOME LATER!

CHAPTER XI   EXPENSES

A. TAXES

You must pay Federal and State income taxes quarterly unless the taxes are withheld by your employer. If you have any earned income where taxes are not withheld, you are responsible for paying the quarterly payments. This is usually estimated by an accountant.

Property taxes may be included in your home mortgage payments along with interest and principal, or billed separately. Due dates for property taxes are half on December 10th, and half on April 10th. Due dates of other city and county taxes depend upon the state and the area in which you live.

B. INTEREST

Real estate interest is usually included in the monthly mortgage payment. At year's end, the lending institution will send you a statement showing total interest paid, amount applied to the principal and the balance owed. If you have owned your home for a few years you have probably built up some property equity. Equity is the amount of the appraised value less the mortgage amount still due. After 1991 you cannot deduct auto loan interest, credit card interest or life insurance loan interest from your income tax. Since you CAN deduct interest on a mortgage equity loan (using that money for whatever you wish) it has become very popular.

C. MEDICAL EXPENSES

All medical expenses including doctors, hospitals, labs, dental and eye care and health insurance premiums are only tax deductible as a percentage (7.5% in 1990) deduction from your adjusted gross income. For example, if your adjusted gross income is $35,000 your medical deductible is $2,625 (35,000 x .075) and you can only deduct non-reimbursed medical expenses from your tax report in excess of $2,625.

D. CONTRIBUTIONS

Under the 1990 tax law, there are two types of deductions. One is the actual cash contribution made to legal charities or churches. The other is non-cash contributions such as donations of clothing, appliances, furniture, etc., to Goodwill, Purple Heart, Salvation Army or other charities. Your accountant will advise you on how this area relates to your tax report.

E. RENTAL AGREEMENTS

After the death of a spouse occurs, many widows and widowers want to sell their homes and rent an apartment or a condominium. Do not be too hasty in making this decision. You may want to rent out your home. You may also have a second or vacation home to rent. However, rental agreements, whether on a month-to-month basis or on a term lease, can present problems.

SOME ITEMS TO BE AWARE OF ARE AS FOLLOWS:

a. CANCELLATION NOTICES
   Who can cancel? Notice time?
   Other eviction rules.

b. PETS & CHILDREN
   Are they allowed? (Size & ages)

c. REPAIRS
   Who pays for what and is it in writing?

d. UTILITIES
   Who pays? Most often, the tenant pays all utilities except water and trash pickup.

e. USE OF GARAGE, CARPORT, ETC.
   Any restrictions?

f. GENERAL UPKEEP OF GROUNDS
  Landlords usually maintain, but be sure
  it is in writing.

g. PLUMBING AND ELECTRICAL
  Can rent be withheld until repairs are made?

h. LATE PAYMENTS
  Penalty and amounts.

i. LANDLORD ENTRANCE
  Clause about your rights.

j. OVERNIGHT PARKING & GUESTS
  Be sure you understand rules.
  Check on guest parking.

k. RESTRICTIONS: SMOKING, ETC.
  List of those that apply.

l. CLEANING & SECURITY DEPOSIT
  List of existing stains, scratches, etc.

m. MAXIMUM NUMBER OF PEOPLE
  Restrictions and evictions.

n. SUBLETTING
  Permission of landlord.

MOST RENTAL LAWS ARE SIMILAR, BUT THERE ARE
VARIATIONS AMONG STATES. BE SURE YOU CHECK
STATE LAWS WHEN YOU MOVE TO A NEW STATE.

NOTES, CHANGES AND UPDATES

CHAPTER XII   MONTHLY CASH FLOW

A. AREAS OF INCOME

HUSBAND'S SALARY	$_____
WIFE'S SALARY	$_____
INTEREST INCOME	$_____
DIVIDENDS	$_____
ALIMONY	$_____
CHILD SUPPORT	$_____
NOTE PROCEEDS (INT. & PRIN.)	$_____
COMMISSIONS	$_____
COMPANY RETIREMENT INCOME	$_____
SPOUSE RETIREMENT INCOME	$_____
SOCIAL SECURITY (HUSBAND)	$_____
SOCIAL SECURITY (WIFE)	$_____
IRA & KEOGH PLAN WITHDRAWALS	$_____
PROPERTY INCOME	$_____
LIMITED PARTNERSHIPS	$_____
NET BUSINESS INCOME	$_____
DISABILITY INCOME	$_____
ROYALTIES	$_____
TRUST FUND	$_____

NOTES, CHANGES AND UPDATES

OTHER INCOME $_____

TOTAL MONTHLY GROSS $_____

You might want to make a note on the opposite page
of the amount of any deductions from salaries, social
security (FICA), insurance premiums, retirement, savings,
government bonds and any others.

B. POSSIBLE EXPENDITURES

MORTGAGE PAYMENT
  (PRIN. & INT.) $_____

MORTGAGE INSURANCE $_____

PROPERTY TAXES $_____

SECOND HOME
  (GROSS PAYMENTS) $_____

MONTHLY RENT
  (IF NO MORTGAGE) $_____

ELECTRIC $_____

GAS $_____

WATER & GARBAGE $_____

TELEPHONES $_____

PEST CONTROL $_____

GARDENER $_____

POOL SERVICE $_____

TV CABLE SERVICE $_____

CLEANING $_____

AIR & HEAT SERVICE $_____

NOTES, CHANGES AND UPDATES

ASSOCIATION DUES $_____

CREDIT CARDS $_____

DEPT. STORES $_____

AUTO LOANS $_____

AUTO LICENCES $_____

AUTO GAS AND OIL $_____

AUTO REPAIRS $_____

AUTO INSURANCE $_____

FOOD & STAPLES $_____

CLOTHING $_____

LIFE INSURANCE $_____

MEDICAL INSURANCE $_____

ACCOUNTANT'S FEES $_____

LEGAL FEES $_____

ALIMONY $_____

CHILD CARE OR SUPPORT $_____

PERSONAL CARE $_____

EDUCATION $_____

MEMBERSHIPS $_____

IRA/KEOGH/RETIREMENT
    CONTRIBUTIONS $_____

GIFTS/CHARITY $_____

INVESTMENTS $_____

OTHER SAVINGS $_____

INCOME TAXES (INCL. FICA) $_____

RECREATION $_____

NOTES, CHANGES AND UPDATES

MAGAZINES & NEWSPAPERS $_____

NOTES PAYABLE $_____

EXPECTED TRAVEL
   EXPENSES $_____

FORCED SAVINGS $_____

MISCELLANEOUS $_____

**TOTAL MONTHLY
EXPENDITURES** $_____

If you are under any deferred compensation plan, this might be a good place to make a note about it, and even keep records of the current accumulation amount.

(If your income is not adequate, find areas where you can reduce or eliminate expenditures.)

PLANNING FOR
THE FUTURE

(THESE COMMENTS ARE FOR REFERENCE ONLY. FOR ALL LEGAL AND TAX MATTERS IT IS BEST TO SEE YOUR PERSONAL TAX ADVISOR.)

A. WILLS

It is amazing how many intelligent people who own a business, have high incomes and dependent families, fail to create or update a will. If your spouse is now deceased, it is essential that you review and make necessary changes in your will, or create one if you have not already done so.

If a person dies without a will, the court will appoint a guardian for minor children. Children become wards of the court until a decision is made regarding guardianship, and the court charges for this service. Obviously, it is imperative for you to **HAVE A WILL**.

In our complex society, with conflicting laws and an ever changing economy, it is astounding that so many people talk about a will but take no action. If you die without a will (intestate), your property is disposed of according to the laws of the state in which the property is located. You must be of sound mind when a will or codicil (supplement or change) is made. You should have a will drawn by an attorney. If you cannot afford an attorney, most stationery stores have legal forms for simple wills. Having a professional draw a will helps to guarantee the protection of inheritance rights of families. Hand-written holograph wills can sometimes create problems.

Your will should be reviewed now and every two years, particularly if there have been many changes such as a family death, children reaching age 25, etc. Be sure that when you update your will, you also review your choice of executor or back-up executor. Having a will and a Family Revocable Living Trust allows assets to be distributed to those heirs whom you designate without probate. Speak to your attorney about a TAX-WISE WILL; attention to tax ramifications can preserve many thousands of dollars.

DRAWING A WILL SHOULD BE YOUR NUMBER ONE PRIORITY

B. LEGAL NEEDS

Many people are afraid of attorneys. Having an attorney and knowing a little about the law is very important. Today people sue for almost any reason. Ignorance of the law is no excuse and you could be heavily penalized.

Laws vary from state to state, so be sure to check your state regulations. There are many specialty fields in law. A good personal attorney will put you in contact with someone who can handle your particular problem if it is not in his or her area of expertise.

You should consult an attorney as one of your help team members when doing any estate planning, drawing your will, signing legal papers, buying and selling property, signing loan documents or suing someone for damages or injury. Find an attorney with whom you feel comfortable. You should be able to communicate easily. Understand the attorney's limitations. Be sure you understand the fee schedule. Be honest and patient when discussing any problem.

Even if you have created a very small estate, be smart and see that it passes on to those **you designate,** not to the state or someone else.

What Is Probate Administration?

Probate brings a will before the court to prove its validity. Probate administration gives creditors of the deceased the opportunity to file claims before the estate is distributed to heirs. Without a will, probate costs can be more expensive.

Here Is What Happens To Your Estate At Death!

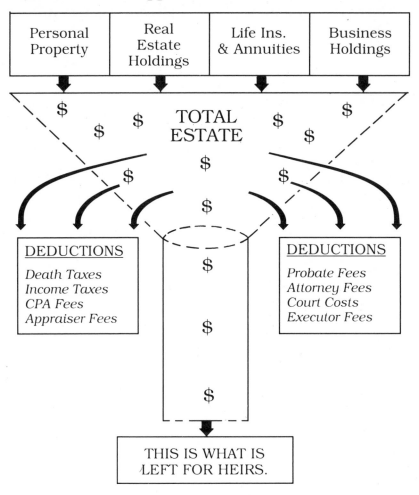

| Personal Property | Real Estate Holdings | Life Ins. & Annuities | Business Holdings |

TOTAL ESTATE

DEDUCTIONS
Death Taxes
Income Taxes
CPA Fees
Appraiser Fees

DEDUCTIONS
Probate Fees
Attorney Fees
Court Costs
Executor Fees

THIS IS WHAT IS LEFT FOR HEIRS.

C. PROBATE

When a death occurs and probate is opened, an estate social security number is issued. This is used from that point on, not the social security number of the deceased. Probate is a procedure that brings a will before the court to prove its validity. It also allows creditors to file claims. Probate usually costs about 5% of the estate value. Holding property in joint tenancy does not necessarily avoid probate. This could create an income tax disadvantage in states which have a community property law. Life insurance is usually not included in probate when there is a named beneficiary.

If there is a probate the attorney will provide you with **Letters Testamentary** which is the legal form appointing an executor in accordance with the will. Certified copies of this form are used to take to banks and elsewhere to prove that the executor is the personal representative of the deceased and authorized to administer the estate under the Independent Administration of Estates Act.

D. FAMILY REVOCABLE TRUST

One of the best ways to eliminate probate is to have a **Family Revocable Living Trust.** If both spouses are alive and if there is a reasonable amount of assets in a variety of investments, it would be worthwhile to ask your attorney about this type of trust. This is a way to avoid probate and many hundreds of dollars in attorney fees after either or both spouses die. There is no loss of asset control and it is not expensive when compared with the benefits afforded. Property of your choice is placed in the trust and held for the benefit of both spouses.

As trustees, you control all assets of the trust. Upon a death, the surviving spouse becomes sole trustee and continues as before without the hassle of legal fees and asset name changes. This type of trust provides complete privacy. No one knows what you had or who inherited it. The beneficiary can collect insurance proceeds payable to the trust, and can use these funds without court approval. See your attorney for any disadvantages.

E. TRUSTS

If you have no investment experience and you inherit over $100,000, along with other assets to manage, you may want to set up a trust which will handle everything during your lifetime.

See your tax advisors, trust attorney or a bank trust officer.

You may also want to talk this over with your accountant. Trusts can provide financial security for your spouse, children and grandchildren. There are also reliable financial counseling firms that you may want to talk to before you make any final decisions in this area. It all depends on the size and complexity of your estate and your financial desires.

F. VITAL ORGANS

Many people wish to make their vital organs available or donate their bodies for medical research. If you wish to do this, obtain a donor card, fill it out and carry it with you. Some states allow you to declare your desires on your driver's license. Close relatives and your doctor should be notified of your intentions. You may wish to include this desire in your will.

G. LIVING WILL

You may want to consider filling out a "Living Will Directive," the form needed to instruct your doctor not to use artificial methods to extend the natural process of dying. The directive is a method, recognized under California law, (and some other states), by which a physician may respect a patient's instruction to permit an imminent death to proceed naturally. A sample appears below. Check to see if your state has the same type of law.

DIRECTIVE TO PHYSICIANS

DIRECTIVE MADE THIS....................DAY OF .... YEAR.................

I,........................being of sound mind, willfully, and voluntarily make known my desire that my life shall not be artificially prolonged under the circumstances set forth below, do hereby declare:

1. If at any time I should have an incurable injury, disease, or illness certified to be a terminal condition by two physicians, and where the application of life sustaining procedures would serve only to artificially prolong the moment of my death and where my physician determines that my death is imminent whether or not life sustaining procedures are utilized, I direct that such procedures be withheld or withdrawn, and that I be permitted to die naturally.

2. In the absence of my ability to give directions regarding the use of such life sustaining procedures, it is my intention that this directive shall be honored by my family and physicians as the final expression of my legal right to refuse medical or surgical treatment and accept the consequences from such refusal.

3. If I have been diagnosed as pregnant and that diagnosis is known to my physician, this directive shall have no force or effect during the course of my pregnancy.

4. I have been diagnosed and notified at least 14 days ago as having a terminal condition by ..................M.D. I understand that if I have not filled in the physician's name, it shall be presumed that I did not have a terminal condition when I made out this directive.

5. This directive shall have no force or effect after 5 years from this date filled in above.

6. I understand the full impact of this directive and I am emotionally and mentally competent to make this directive.

SIGNED........................

The declarant has been known to me and I believe him or her to be of sound mind.

WITNESS..............WITNESS..................

H. DURABLE POWER OF ATTORNEY

Now that you have filled out the living will form on the previous page, you should consider obtaining and filling out a DURABLE POWER OF ATTORNEY FOR HEALTH CARE. This is a document that a person signs stating that if they are unable to make health decisions, the person nominated on the form will have the power to make the decisions for them. This form can usually be obtained from the stationery stores or from some of the hospitals.

NOTES, CHANGES AND UPDATES

CHAPTER XIV   FUNERAL ARRANGEMENTS

NOW, while you are alive and healthy, is the time to sit down with your spouse and plan as much of your funeral arrangements as possible. You also might want to select a burial place, funeral home or crematory, depending on your desires. Go back to Chapter I of this handbook and it will help guide you through some of the necessary steps. Fill out the following chart listing your choice of pall bearers.

HUSBAND'S CHOICE: WIFE'S CHOICE:

1._____   1._____

2._____   2._____

3._____   3._____

4._____   4._____

5._____   5._____

6._____   6._____

At a funeral there is usually a special place set aside for the immediate family. The pall bearers usually sit with other family members in the first few rows. These arrangements should be made with the funeral director.

CHAPTER XV   SOCIAL SECURITY

If you are age 60 or over and your spouse is deceased and he or she was covered under the Social Security program, you are probably eligible for survivor benefits. IF A SURVIVOR RECEIVES A SOCIAL SECURITY CHECK PAYABLE TO THE DECEASED IT SHOULD NOT BE CASHED. RETURN IT TO THE SOCIAL SE-CURITY ADMINISTRATION.

At age 62, covered persons may elect early retirement and receive Social Security benefits. You may also be eligible for early retirement if you are totally disabled. If you are still working you may wish to defer taking retirement if your income exceeds the allowable amount at the time you want to retire. In 1990 the law was changed so that a person receiving Social Security benefits loses only one dollar for every three dollars earned.

At age 70 you may earn any amount and still draw Social Security benefits. If you are under age 70 and your personal earned income is over the limits set by Social Security each year, then you may lose part or all of those benefits. If you do, a spouse who is receiving benefits attributed to those earnings will also lose those benefits. The amounts and qualifications for all benefits are available through the Social Security Administration.

To receive benefits, call your local Social Security office. Remember, Social Security benefits are not automatic...**you must apply for them.** You should apply for benefits about three months prior to date of eligibility.

The amount you pay for Social Security has been changed many times. There will be more changes in the future and that is the reason it is important to pick up a free handbook at your local Social Security office.

CHAPTER XVI   MEDICARE

Medicare rules have been changed frequently in the past, and will probably continue to be changed in the future. Pick up a current Medicare handbook at any Social Security office. About three months before your sixty-fifth birthday, you should apply for your Medicare benefits. Part A, hospital and drug expenses, is automatically provided. You are entitled to unlimited hospitalization for approved care after you pay a single annual deductible. Benefit periods and co-insurance payments, or "reserve days" have been eliminated. You can also have up to 150 days in a skilled nursing care facility without a hospital stay. Beginning in 1990 home health care has been improved. You can now have an unlimited number of days of hospice care.

You must ask and **apply for part B,** doctor and out-patient benefits. Many changes took place beginning January 1, 1990. These benefits were greatly improved. Your share of approved charges for services and supplies covered by medical insurance will be limited to $1,370; this will increase annually. You will continue to be required to pay for the first $75 (deductible) of charges approved by Medicare and 20 percent of all approved charges after that until these out-of-pocket expenses total $1,370. It does not matter whether these expenses are paid directly by you or by your private insurance company. There are additional benefits listed in the Medicare handbook.

Because Medicare does not pay 100% of hospital bills, doctor bills or other services, you should have a supplement that picks up part or all of the Medicare deductibles and co-insurance. Premiums for Medicare are taken out of your monthly Social Security check. Some companies provide this supplement for you when you retire. If not, get one from a reliable insurance company or an H.M.O. Premiums for this additional coverage are very expensive and run about $70 to $90 per individual on a monthly basis. There are many companies selling this coverage, so you should shop around and be sure of what coverage is being provided. **You only need one supplemental plan!**

CHAPTER XVII   DISPOSITION OF PERSONAL PROPERTY

Upon death, there are usually many items that have to be given away, sold or disposed of in some way. There are jewelry items, art objects, stamp and coin collections, furniture and appliances, clothing and many more. Now is the time to sit down and write a note in this handbook as to your desires.

Disposition of some items are expressed in the will, others are only verbal desires expressed between spouses and/or children. If you have certain jewelry items, art objects or even stamp or coin collections, make a note here in this handbook, so that the survivors will know what you desired.

Examine this list carefully. Consider distributing or disposing of certain items NOW.

Also, make a note of how you want your executor to dispose of certain other valuable items. If they are to be sold, explain approximately what value can be expected and suggestions of who to contact for help. When you find out what needs to be done to dispose of the items, make a note in this handbook.

Many items can be sold through advertising in the newspaper. Others may have to be sold through "used outlets" or large national purchasing companies that go around the country buying all types of items. Depending on the situation, some items may be given to charity and used as a tax deduction.

The main action that you must take now, is to put your current thoughts down in writing, by making notes across from the listed items in Chapter VI. Do not leave your heirs in the dark!

NOTES, CHANGES AND UPDATES

CHAPTER XVIII   WHEN DEATH IS IMMINENT

This is a difficult subject to discuss, but there is no sense in procrastination if the wishes of your loved ones are to be carried out. Therefore, if you are living with someone who is terminally ill or who is mentally incapacitated, then you need to take several steps **NOW.**

1. If the person is coherent, try to fill out all of the areas of this handbook as quickly as possible.

2. Review the will and be sure that all the items, instructions and wishes are current. If not add a codicil.

3. If necessary, obtain a power of attorney (also called power of appointment).

4. If you have not already done so, plan the funeral arrangements. Go through the steps as shown in Chapter I.

5. If you feel it is appropriate to ask the dying spouse his or her wishes for the funeral, you should decide the type of ceremony, type of casket, the clothing, and any other special wishes.

6. You may want to set up a standby trust. The trust ends if the disability ceases.

7. Talk to your professional help team to see what other actions you should consider.

DO NOT PUT OFF TAKING ACTION. DO IT NOW!

NOTES, CHANGES AND UPDATES

Appendix

SERVICE AND UTILITY LIST

Here is a sample name change list. You can have it readily accessible when and if you move, or if you wish to change the ownership or billing services.

RESIDENCE MORTGAGEE   PHONE_____

RESIDENCE MORTGAGEE   PHONE_____

TAX COLLECTOR   PHONE_____

INSURANCE COMPANIES:

1.   PHONE_____

2.   PHONE_____

BURGLAR ALARM CO.   PHONE_____

ASSOCIATION OFFICE   PHONE_____

GAS COMPANY   PHONE_____

TELEPHONE CO.   PHONE_____

CITY UTILITIES   PHONE_____

COUNTY UTILITIES   PHONE_____

PEST CONTROL   PHONE_____

TV CABLE SERVICE   PHONE_____

POOL SERVICE CO.   PHONE_____

GARAGE DOOR CO.   PHONE_____

GARDENER   PHONE_____

NEWSPAPER & MAGAZINES:

1.   PHONE_____

2.   PHONE_____

3.   PHONE_____

CREDIT CARD COMPANIES:

1.   PHONE_____

2.   PHONE_____

3.   PHONE_____

4.   PHONE_____

SOCIAL CLUBS:

1.   PHONE_____

2.   PHONE_____

3.   PHONE_____

GYM OR WORKOUT CO.   PHONE_____

MOTOR VEHICLE DEPT.   PHONE_____

AUTO INSURANCE CO.   PHONE_____

BANKS:

1.   PHONE_____

2.   PHONE_____

3.   PHONE_____

INVESTMENT COMPANIES:

1.   PHONE_____

2.   PHONE_____

3.   PHONE_____

CREDIT UNIONS:

1.   PHONE_____

2.   PHONE_____

OTHERS:

1.   PHONE_____

2.   PHONE_____

Appendix

MAIN DOCUMENT LOCATION LIST

ITEM   **LOCATION**

ADOPTION PAPERS_____

ANNUITY POLICIES_____

AGREEMENTS_____

ART OBJECTS_____

BANK BOOKS_____

BANK STATEMENTS_____

BIRTH CERTIFICATES_____

CASH OR TRAVELER'S CHECKS_____

CEMETERY PLOT OR CRYPT_____

CITIZENSHIP PAPERS_____

CHURCH MEMBERSHIPS_____

CLUB MEMBERSHIPS_____

COIN COLLECTION_____

COPYRIGHTS_____

CREDIT UNIIONS_____

DEEDS_____

DIVORCE PAPERS_____

DRIVERS' LICENSES_____

DURABLE POWER OF ATTORNEY_____

EXPENSES PAID_____

FAMILY REVOCABLE LIVING TRUST_____

ITEM	LOCATION

FUNERAL ARRANGEMENTS_____

HOME INVENTORY_____

INCOME STATEMENTS
  (Current Year)_____

INCOME TAX PAPERS
  (old)_____

INCOME TAX PAPERS
  (Current Year)_____

IRA ACCOUNTS_____

INSURANCE

  LIFE_____

  HEALTH_____

  DISABILITY_____

  HOMEOWNERS_____

  AUTO_____

  COMPUTER_____

INVESTMENTS_____

KEOGH ACCOUNT_____

LEASES_____

LIVING WILL_____

MARITAL CERTIFICATE_____

MILITARY RECORDS_____

MORTGAGES_____

NOTES RECEIVABLE_____

NOTES PAYABLE_____

ITEM	LOCATION

PAID BILLS
  (Current year)_____

PASSPORTS_____

PATENTS_____

PENSION PLANS_____

PET RECORDS_____

RECEIPTS_____

RENTAL AGREEMENTS_____

SAFE DEPOSIT BOX_____

SECURITIES_____

SOCIAL SECURITY_____

STAMP COLLECTION_____

TAX PAPERS_____

TRADEMARKS_____

TRUSTS_____

VEHICLE OWNERSHIP PAPERS

     PINK SLIPS_____

     FINANCE PAPERS_____

WARRANTIES_____

WILLS_____

NOTES, CHANGES AND UPDATES

Appendix

GLOSSARY

ITEM	EXPLANATION
ANNUITY	Return of investment now or in the future.
ASSETS	Items that can usually be converted into money.
BROKER	One who buys or sells for another for a commission.
C.D.	Bank or Savings & Loan Certificate of Deposit
C.L.U.	Chartered Life Underwriter. Professional Designation in the Life Insurance Industry
C.P.A.	Certified Public Accountant
CODICIL	Supplement or addition to a will.
DEFERRED COMP.	Employer defers compensation until a later date.
DEFINED BENEFIT	A type of retirement plan where the amount to be paid at retirement is funded in advance.
FAMILY REVOCABLE LIVING TRUST	Living trust created while alive, holding assets outside probate.
F.I.C.A.	Federal Insurance Compensation Act (Social Security)

H.M.O.	Health Maintenance Organization
IRA	Individual Retirement Plan
IRS	Internal Revenue Service
KEOGH	HR-10 Retirement plan for self employed.
LIABILITIES	Debts or obligations
LIMITED PARTNERSHIP	Investment where you as a limited partner are not liable for acts of General partners.
JOINT VENTURE	A special type of partnership.
LIVING WILL	Form expressing desire NOT to use artificial methods to extend natural process of dying.
MONEY PURCHASE	A type of retirement plan where money is deposited to buy a deferred annuity.
MORTGAGE	A conditional transfer of property pledged as security for the repayment of a loan.
NET WORTH	Total assets minus total liabilities.
PROBATE	Process to check the validity of a will. Proof of assets passing through court.
PROFIT SHARING PLAN	Employer retirement plan based on profits of the company.

S & L	Savings & Loan
TRUST	Custody and care of assets.
VA	Veterans Administration
WILL	The legal document of giving or bequeathing.
W2	Employee income reporting form.
401K	Employer-Employee tax deferred investment plan.
1098	Form given by mortgage lender on interest paid.
1099	Form given by employers to report income.
K1	An income tax reporting form sent to investors.

NOTES, CHANGES AND UPDATES